Haiku! *Gesundheit*

an illustrated collection of ridiculous haiku poetry

by Ross Venokur

illustrated by Kenny Scharf

SIMON & SCHUSTER
new york london toronto sydney singapore

For Jason and Danielle:

What in the world would
the Dog-Faced Boy be without
Goat Boy and Damsmell?

For Keith Haring

—R. V.   —K. S.

INTRODUCTION

Haiku is an ancient Japanese art form that allows the poet to capture a snapshot of the extraordinary in life's ordinary moments. The strict but elegant form of haiku—three lines whose syllables total five, then seven, then five—complements the beauty of the thought. Haiku can be a way for the poet to express the wonder of a sunset, or how that single tiger lily by the road changed his life, or how he felt the first time he removed his own head and used it as a bowling ball.

The world has long feared that haiku died with its original masters, Matsuo Basho, Yosa Buson, Kobayashi Issa, and Masaoka Shiki. However, *Haiku! Gesundheit* introduces the world to the new masters of this ancient art, Ross Venokur and Kenny Scharf.

Little boys named Art

who do not know how to paint

wonder why they're Art.

Rossi the

scuttled around

and barked at the

dog-boy
on all fours
moon.

Tiny little men
residing in Hoboken
got stepped on today.

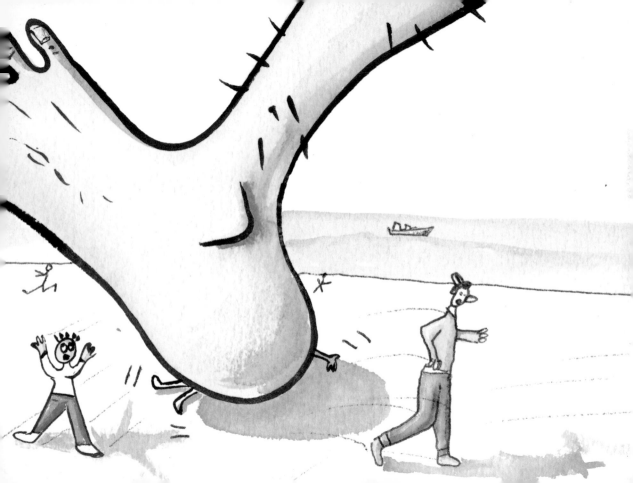

One two three four five

I proclaim we're all alive—

except for *that* guy.

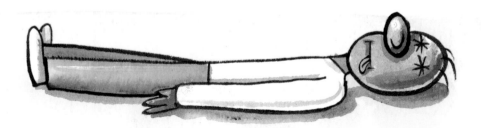

Marty picked his

shoved his finger

it came out his

nose—

so far up,

ear.

Anne dreamed of eggplants.
Then, one day, she became one.
Now she dreams of kids.

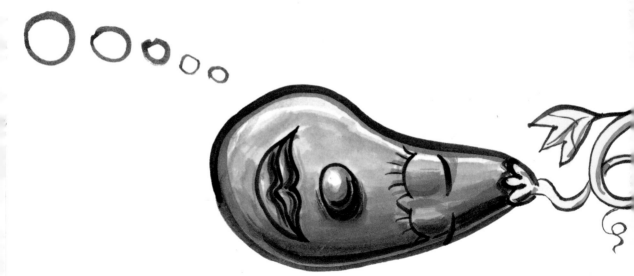

Anteater inhaled

a beetle who objected—

"Hey man, I'm no ant!"

Doughnuts are de-lish
just as long as you eat them,
and they don't eat you.

Driving in his car,
Mr. Hendrix realized
he was on a yak.

Drill three holes in head.

Remove head from your body.

It's time to go bowl!

Broken arms and legs
can be a major nuisance
when riding a horse.

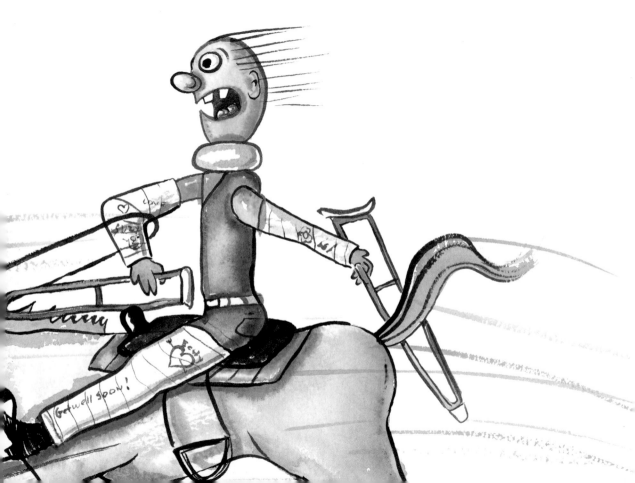

A vacuum cleaner

picked up Sam and said to him:

"*You* eat all that dirt!"

A man named

was so incredibly

except for his

Oswald
bald—
toes.

When brushing your hair,
it is best to use a comb,
not a lawn mower.

Tom Television

swapped head with TV—now needs

a mirror to see.

Flying over town,
Beth saw a boy she hated
and spit on his head.

On Halloween night,
Billy dressed as a tuba—
blew the rest away.

Haiku poetry.

Poetry or poet tree?

Words where buds should be.

SIMON & SCHUSTER BOOKS FOR YOUNG READERS
An imprint of Simon & Schuster Children's Publishing
Division
1230 Avenue of the Americas, New York, New York 10020

SIMON & SCHUSTER BOOKS FOR YOUNG READERS is a trademark of
Simon & Schuster.

Book design by Lee Wade
The text of this book is set in Meta Book.
The illustrations are rendered in watercolor.
Printed in Hong Kong
10 9 8 7 6 5 4 3 2 1
Library of Congress Card Number: 00-105046
ISBN 0-689-84044-6